SOLITARY CONFINEMENT

(MY WALLS ARE TALKING)

DAMON SMITH

Solitary Confinement

(My walls are talking)

These thoughts are only a small piece of
what goes through my mind when I am all
by myself, and they are not meant to hurt
or discourage the reader. They are only meant
to enlighten those in the free-world of the thoughts
hopes, dreams, fears, and concerns of those
of us on the other side of the fence.

In Honor of a Strong Mother

At 7:29 on 11/29/2017, my mother, Edna Jean Smith finally lost her long battle with the autoimmune disease multiple sclerosis. In her honor, the @BaconMSpig was founded to give charitable donations to deserving sufferers of MS. (Feed the pig)

A portion of the sales of this book will be donated to the foundation.

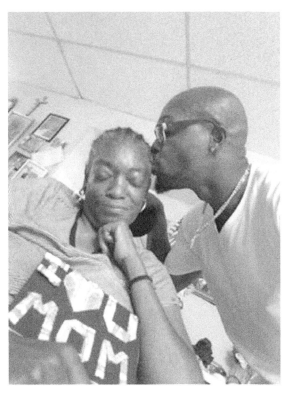

Table of Contents

1. (Difficult)
2. Sojourn
3. Truth
4. Feel Me
5. Intuition
6. Hurt
7. Mother
8. Window
9. Free Time
10. Faulty
11. Words
12. Answers
13. Déjà vu
14. Edna
15. Never Again
16. Genuine
17. In My Corner
18. Proof
19. Escape
20. Solution
21. Granny
22. Specific
23. Anguish
24. Unrealistic
25. Today
26. Recognition
27. Patient
28. Perfect
29. Mirage
30. Principle
31. Celebration
32. Street Life
33. Unconditional
34. Mixed Emotions
35. Here
36. Collect Call
37. Lil Dirty
38. Second Chance
39. The Block
40. (The First and Last Letter)
41. Who Will Be There
42. Younger Brother
43. Chess
44. Opposites
45. 7-House
46. Secrets
47. Alternate
48. Freedom
49. Education
50. Vision
51. Know It All

52. Imagination
53. Comrade
54. Your Worth
55. Forgiveness
56. Present & Past
57. 99 Problems
58. The Institution
59. Actual Friend
60. EJS
61. Clarity
62. Silence
63. Conversation
64. Love One
65. Assurance
66. Everyday
67. Friend
68. Love Bird
69. Pain
70. Wisdom
71. Where's the Love?
72. Water
73. Perception
74. History
75. Momma
76. Recidivist
77. Prison
78. (Lady Abstract)

Difficult

  This is the hardest letter I ever had to write in my life. Because I remember the days and nights when you used to hold me so tight. You showed me the meaning of love unconditionally. My love for you was divided, between you and the streets. I wish I could change the things that happened, but that's only a dream. And it's harder to be away from you than I make it seem. I can count on one hand the times you came up to visit. And on the other, I can add up all your letters and pictures. I broke my promise, and it hurts that you won't let me forget it. It's to the point that I don't think that you will ever forgive me. Saying "I'm sorry" ain't enough, then tell me what I should do? Because I'm fresh out of ideas, plus I'm lost and confused. I put myself in this position, but I'm lonely without you. And not a day goes by that I'm not thinking about you. What we had was more than physical lust. It was more mental with us, a combination of commitment and trust. I love you more than these words can explain, but I'm through playing this game, because I'm tired of the heart ache and pain. I never asked you for anything that you couldn't give. So, was it too much, when I asked for you to just keep it real? I loved you and I showed it more than I ever said it. My mistake was in the past, now it's affecting the present. I'm looking forward to the future, if you with me or not, plus I got another woman that can fill in your spot. She's only half of what you are, but half is better than nothing. And she understands, that prison comes with being a hustler. I never told you what I did, because I loved you too much. And I didn't think that it would matter that I stuck niggas up. It never stopped you from asking me for this and that, so where the money came from is an irrelevant fact. I didn't think you needed to know that I made niggas bleed. I wanted you to be safe from the pull of the streets. You were young and naïve, and I really wanted you to stay pure. I was rotten to the core, and loving you was the cure.

  I showed you a side of me that no one else ever saw. I was comfortable in your presence with my skills and my flaws. I was there whenever you called, because my love was complete. I was everything that you needed, from the streets to the sheets. I satisfied your every need, no matter how small or big. But there were consequences that came with the way I lived. I never meant to come to jail, but that's the way that it is. And I know that leaving you hurt, but do you know how I feel? Just imaging the one you love the most not loving you back. And the times you need them the most, they're just not pulling the slack. Then add to that all the lies they tell, and all their excuses. And you will probably have a clue of how the fuck I've been doing. I ain't mad at you in the least, I blame myself for the problem. And I'm glad I figured it out, because I know how to solve it. I can do bad by myself, I don't need your assistance. So please forget you ever knew me and deny my existence.

  It was fun while it lasted, and I'm sorry I'm bouncing. But when I needed you the most you weren't there when it counted. I shed tears writing this letter, but it won't happen again. And I pray that you can find another man that can do what I did!

<u>Sojourn</u>

I was cuffed and chained,
      just to go on a visit.

To see my aunt and little brother,
      I was punished and privileged.

Hand cuffed, belly chained,
      with the leg shackles to match.

Fully restrained inside a booth,
      so I can talk through a crack.

Happy to see my family,
      but I hate how I look.

Years away from a crime,
      but I look like a crook.

Solitary confinement,
      the punishment's consequence.

Treated just like an animal,
      when consequence contradicts.

<u>Truth</u>

I heard an inmate say yesterday,
    that he don't wish this on his enemies,
        but I could hear the lie in his voice.

What he said truly offended me,
    because he didn't understand that prison's a mental injury,
        and worse than a physical.

These walls and fences,
    hurt more than bullets and knives,
        because these places just punish the mind.

If words could describe the pain felt,
    from losing years at a time,
        people would stop wishing their enemies die.

Instead they would pray,
    that all their enemies get caught and confined,
        so they can understand what death is and still be alive.

Feel Me

How can you claim to feel my pain,
when you ain't walked a mile in my shoes?

Seen what I seen, did what I did,
been through the stuff I been through.

So, empathy's reserved,
for those that really did this.

Unless you been here,
you'll never feel the pain I live with.

You'll never understand,
how I think, move, and react.

So, your empathy is sympathy,
and I don't need that.

Intuition

How many times can I apologize,
    for coming to jail?

When I was told by 21,
    that I'd be here or in hell.

That was at eleven or twelve,
    now I'm 29 and stuck in a cell.

So you can say,
    I did exactly what my Momma'em said.

Been gone ten,
    and got another ten before I see the crib.

And I pray that all they say,
    is I won't come back again.

Hurt

Sometimes I want to cry, but I can't get the tears to come from my eyes. I been gone too many calendars, I'm stuck in my pride. Everything I did to survive, keeps my pain deep inside. To the point I couldn't even feel it when my grandfather died. I didn't even know he was gone, until some years had gone by. So, I tattooed him on my arm, so he always by my side. Lost my uncle to getting high, and more than ten of my guys. And I swear I can see their faces, when I look at the sky. Really think I'm losing my mind, from doing all this time. And the longer that I'm confined, the hurt inside become much harder to hide. So much in fact, that every day I think about suicide. And how the world might be a better place, if I weren't alive.

Mother

If I wrote a list of reasons I love you,
    it could make it to the sun and back,
        even further, if I didn't use the front and back.

Words can't describe the way I feel,
    when it comes to you,
        and they can't say the things I do, did, and done for you.

There's nothing in this world,
    that means more to me than you,
        not even self, because I will leave if you need me to.

It's more than love,
    it's admiration, loyalty, and respect,
        because you gave me something that I could never give to myself.

Window

Looking at life through a hole in the fence.

So far away, but so close that I can see where I been.

Razor wire cutting my hopes into pieces of lint.

Seen my dreams electrocuted climbing over the fence.

Mind, body, and soul confined in a place full of sin.

Praying that I can see the streets, so I can fully repent.

Apologize for every law I broke and rule that I bent.

To show the world that I can learn from the mistakes I commit.

Stuck in between a rock and hard place with nowhere to twist.

Counting up each and everything I had that I really miss.

One into two, two into three, all the way up to ten.

I'm on the inside looking out, wondering who is looking in.

<u>Free Time</u>

The only way to describe my thoughts, is a complicated process. Covering everything that I survey that ain't on nonsense. Past, present, and future, because I learn from my experience. Illusion or reality, feels like I'm an experiment. Placed in different predicaments to see how I can handle them. All types of situations from honesty down to scandalous. Physically confined, but mentally I'm a traveler. Searching for information that I eat up like a scavenger. Knowledge is power, I'm trying to consume as much as possible. So, I can go over, around or through life's little obstacles. Think for myself and others, when circumstances permit it. Understanding of idiots, intolerant of ignorant. All the time in the world, but not a second free for playing. I need every moment I got, because I'm plotting, planning, and waiting.

Faulty

Who needs enemies, when I have to watch the
ones that are friends to me? For ulterior
motives and back-stabbing tendencies.

The ones that want something for nothing on
the regular. The ones that's jealous that
turn into my competitors.

The same friends that tell me they love me
when I'm doing good. The ones that be hard
to find when things don't go the way they should.

The same friends that smile in my face that
really want to frown. The same ones that
talk bad about me when I'm not around.

The ones that's close, that add insult to
every injury. Who needs foes, when friends
act worse than my enemies.

<u>Words</u>

If you listen close enough, you can see who you dealing with.

You can tell by their conversation, who real and who full of shit.

It's more than just what gets said, it's also what's never spoken.

Some word play is confusing, some silence is really golden.

The difference between the two, is so small you can actually miss it.

That's why you have to stay focused and always paying attention.

Most people ain't who they claim to be, they just playing a role.

They pretending to be a character that's just part of the show.

Acting for entertainment, no problem living a lie.

They the types that'll switch positions so quick it'll blow your mind.

On the other side of the coin, is the people that live the truth.

But the problem with hundred proof, is there's only a chosen few.

Rare as a shooting star and precious as every dream.

Is the ones that mean what they say, and the ones that say what they mean.

Answers

If I tell you I'm sorry, would you believe me or think I'm lying?

Hold it against me, even though you know that I'm trying?

If my apologies sincere, would you take it for what it's worth?

Or would you let it go in one ear, and right out of the other first?

Is my past affecting my present, in ways that cannot be fixed?

So much that you won't forgive, and so much you'll never forget?

Is there anything I can do, to change the way you feel about me?

Or is it just a lost cause, since you can live without me?

What about all our memories, are they worth it or worthless?

Or should I let them go, because they're not serving a purpose?

Which way should I go, which way should I show you that I'm different?

Or are you just another thing, I lost because of prison?

Déjà Vu

How can I explain,

what it feels like to be locked in a cage?

When I can't even describe,

how I get through the day.

Seconds, minutes, and hours,

days, weeks, and months.

Years and decades lost,

over things that didn't mean much.

Mind games and violence,

razor wire and fences.

Gun towers and turn-keys,

make up this crooked system.

Same thing every day,

every day is the same too.

Every day is the same thing,

similar to déjà vu.

<u>Edna</u>

I love you, more than cars, more than clothes.

More than diamonds, more than rubies, more than gold.

More than food, more than drugs, more than money.

More than Friday, more than Saturday, more than Sunday.

More than he, more than she, more than them.

More than they, more than her, more than him.

More than up, more than down, more than left.

More than right, more than life, more than death.

More than good, more than bad, more than people.

I love you, more than self, and more than freedom.

Never Again

When you told me you loved me,

I thought that it would last forever,

Because I believed love could get us passed whatever,

But I guess that I was wrong for believing in love,

Or maybe I just was wrong for believing in us.

Genuine

I love you unconditionally, it makes no
difference what the conditions may be.

Good or bad, right or wrong, makes no
difference to me.

I love you no matter what place or position
you see.

Top or bottom, in the middle, or any place
in between.

My love for you will never change no matter
where we should be.

Through ups and downs, and every trial and
tribulation we reach.

The love I have for you, is more than just
a figure of speech.

Through stress and strain, joy and pain,
and everything you can feel.

My love for you is more than a thought,
because my love's really real.

In My Corner

If I counted the reasons I love you,
I would run out of numbers.

Because there's not enough digits,
to count the ways that I love you.

I love you for everything you did,
especially being my mother.

Because without you in my life,
it may have taken me under.

All the advice that you gave me,
plus, your knowledge and wisdom.

All the warnings that you gave me,
to keep me out of the system.

And even though I didn't listen,
it didn't stop you from loving me.

And that's the only thing that matters,
having you where you're supposed to be.

Proof

If you love me the way you say you do,
      then why don't you show me?
Because what you're showing ain't love,
      you treat me like you don't know me.
Did I do something to you,
      to make you make that decision?
Is there something that I can do,
      besides break out of prison?
My love for you hasn't changed,
      it's still the way that it was.
So, I'll suffer through all this pain,
      for my unconditional love.

Escape

I see freedom out of my window,

but it's so far away that I can't touch it.

The closest I get to freedom,

is to think, see, or discuss it.

Locked inside fences,

more trapped than incarcerated.

Watched by the prison staff,

to make sure that nothing works in my favor.

Watched by the population,

so there's no secrets about my movements.

Most ready to tell,

if they can't do the things I'm doing.

The only way to escape,

is to let my thoughts leave the institution.

So I get away in day dreams,

because they're my problem's solution.

Solution

Instead of loving those that love me,
I chose to love those that I loved.

I didn't understand love ain't love,
and water is almost thicker than blood.

It depends on the circumstances,
and the people involved.

It depends on the situation,
and if love gets dissolved.

What was love yesterday,
might not be the same way tomorrow.

What was happy yesterday,
today might turn into sorrow.

Now I see how pretty predicaments,
can turn extremely ugly.

Now I don't love the ones that I love,
I only love the ones that love me.

Granny

Without you,

there would be no her.

Without her,

there would be no me.

I love her

for having me.

And you,

for having she.

Specific

If you stay with me while I'm down,
    then I know that it's love.

    If you leave when things get rough,
        then I know that it's lust.

        If you always tell me the truth,
            then I know we got trust.

            If you lie to me just because,
                then I know it ain't love.

<u>Anguish</u>

      I hurt people that I love,
not physically but mentally.

      And words can't describe,
the pain they go through by missing me.

      All the pain that I'm going through,
by dealing with this misery.

      Is nothing compared to the hurt,
my family felt when they sentenced me.

Unrealistic

What I lost for the love of the streets,
is more than I can ever retrieve.

Every day that I spend in a cell,
makes it harder to breathe.

It's not hard to believe,
that I'll never receive a reprieve.

Everything I've achieved,
that was worth it is worthless to me.

What I lost over greed,
is the reason my family grieves?

I was young and naïve,
influenced by the hustlers and thieves.

Unconscious of the repercussions,
of the web that I weaved.

I lied and deceived,
to satisfy my wants and needs.

Now I wish I was free,
but that's only a hope and a dream.

That my mind can conceive,
during moments reality leaves.

Today

If you leave me,
believe me it gets worse than me.

I was birthed in the streets,
where love and friends are worthless to me.

What's worth it to me,
is money, power, respect and deceit.

They were lessons to me,
that I learned from the test in the streets.

What's a blessing to me,
another day of breaths in the streets.

Because death in the streets,
is the beginning of resting in peace.

No more wins or defeats,
no more falling or planting your feet.

No more pride and conceit,
no more beginning or end of the week.

Recognition

If I see you or not, will never change the way I feel about you.
There's nothing better than you, so I really can't live without you.
You're everything I need, and you're the only thing I want.
You're everything in the back, the middle, and in the front.
You gave me something special, that I can never replace.
You showed me things about life, that I won't forget or erase.
I'm part of you, the same way that you are a part of me.
And that part of me, loves you more than anything I can see.

Patient

From one hole to another, and it's still the same.
As far as the eye can see, there are weirdos and lames.

Words can't describe the situation, no matter the selection.
It's stranger than I ever thought, after the first impression.

Not looking for any trouble, conflict, or altercations.
But it seems that those are the only problems I'll be facing.

It's only a matter of time before the truth will show itself.
So, I'm watching my front, back, and sides while praying for help.

Perfect

The most beautiful thing in this world,
is love without restrictions.

Love without contradictions,
a love without comprehension.

As pure as a mother's love,
understanding without suspicion.

A love without competition,
a love that has no conditions.

An unconditional love,
that promises growth and ambition.

A love built on tradition,
that has no consequences.

Mirage

Can you tell me what the problem is? What did I ever do to you, to make you leave after I caught this bid? Before I got locked up, you showed nothing but love. But now, all I got is memories of kisses and hugs. If I could change the things that happened, I wouldn't. Because now I know the truth about how you really feel for a nigga. Out of sight, out of mind sounds so cliché. But it's the truth that I live and breathe every day. What I thought was love, was really just a misunderstanding. I misinterpreted your words with my delusions of grandeur. I thought you would be around, infinity plus one. But when the gavel hit the table, what was us was done. And that hurt me in a place that takes forever to heal. It broke my heart and the pain I feel is surreal. I will never forget, nor will I ever forgive. There is nothing that you can do, to change the things that you did. Every lie that you told, every promise you never kept. Every visit you missed, every dollar you never sent. Every time that I think about it, I feel more than upset. Because a part of me believes that we were better than that. But I guess I was wrong, truthfully it is what it is. I can think what I want, but things are how they really appear.

Principle

My thoughts of you run the gamut,
from infatuation to lust,
from honesty to trust,
from single to us.

My thoughts of you are motivation
my thoughts of you are inspiration,
my thoughts of you are stimulation
I think of you as medication.

My thoughts of you are filled with appreciation,
my thoughts of you are filled with consideration,
my thoughts of you are filled with emancipations,
I think of you for relaxation.

My thoughts of you are conversations,
my thoughts of you are celebrations,
my thoughts of you are emancipations,
I think of you on a daily basis,
(to get me through my situation).

Celebration

      Words can't describe the joy that I feel inside, with you on our anniversary. They're only words to me, and my emotions can't be summed up in words, because nouns and verbs can't show you my love. They're only a plus, added to how I feel, think, and respond, they only help for me to strengthen our bond. With you in my arms, mental or physical I'm more than complete, and anything that interferes with that is forced to retreat. My love is more than discreet, for you I'll do whatever it takes, wherever the place, whenever the date. Whatever it takes, my love covers it every way that you can think up love, so when I think of love, you're the one that I think of.

Street Life

Take a walk in my shoes,
and see life from a different perspective.

Hang out with the killers,
and the young and the restless.

Play the game by the rules,
following the laws and policies.

Do whatever comes to mind,
without regrets or apologies.

Live life to the fullest,
like every day is the last one.

Don't worry about tomorrow,
because today is a fast one.

Let nothing intervene,
between pleasure and dividends.

Let nothing interfere,
not even family and close-knit friends.

Burn bridges down for fun,
don't care what nobody has to say.

Talk crazy to the world,
run over anything in the way.

Catch cases back to back,
make bond then run until they catch you up.

Then go to jail and prison,
and spend the next ten years trying to make it up.

Unconditional

Who loves me like my momma do? Nobody I can think of. Some love can make it close, but not enough for it to reach hers. Her love is unconditional, and it shows in her actions. No matter what I get in to, and no matter what happens, she's there when I need her, she's there when she doesn't have to be. She takes care of business and finds the time to look after me. Her love seems to be limitless, and I'm glad that I have her. Inside my book of life, she plays a role in every chapter. She knows about the streets, and she know about business. Along with giving birth to me, she also passed down her wisdom. She never lied to me, everything she said was the truth. And even when it hurt, she kept it one hundred proof. There's no one that can match her, she's in a league of her own. That's why I love her like she loves me, because momma can do no wrong.

Mixed Emotions

How can you love me,
when you talk to me with anger and hatred?

Your attitude is so ugly,
it's in need of a facelift.

What did I ever do to you,
to make you act so hateful?

When all I showed was love,
that never crossed or betrayed you.

Who made you that way,
who turned you into an ice-queen?

Who turned you into a monster,
that only cares about nice things?

What happened to the pretty girl,
that played in my day dreams?

Is she lost and forgotten,
except for my many memories?

Will she ever return,
or is my hope a lost cause?

Or should I let it go,
and charge it all to a lost thought?

Here

It hurts more than I can handle,
but pain is a part of life here.

Right here,
depression is part of the day and night here.

Life here,
is more than the tally of wrong and right here.

Nights here,
is just like the strain but people can rest here.

Rest here,
is almost impossible with the stress here.

Test here,
is ten in on twenty and feeling blessed here.

Collect Call

Hearing your voice brought a smile to my face.
When I'm stuck inside of a place where a smile can be a fatal mistake.

The same place where a smile is worn upside down.
Where a smile is rarely seen because it's usually a frown.

And a frown is only worn because it speaks for itself.
It explains the situation without wasting a breath.

But hearing yours changed things for the moments we talked.
And that's one of the reasons I love you with all of my heart.

Lil Dirty

I can tell that my neighbor is lonely by the way that he talks. Everything that he says is somehow just a way of validating his thoughts. He's just a child, and he doesn't understand that life is a game. Sometimes you win, sometimes you lose, depending on how you play. He is so unconscious, I can only blame the way he was raised. Because I see from how he acts, they never taught him the rules of the game. And it's a shame, that it's too late for him to change what they made. So, he gonna be the same way, until he plays in his grave. He got my deepest sympathy, but I can't give him no aid. Since he didn't learn the way I did, he'll have to learn from making mistakes.

<u>Second Chance</u>

How can you tell me that you love me,
    when I ain't seen you in years?

You think writing me now,
    gonna make up for the time you ain't been here?

No visits, no money, no mail,
    in over a decade.

Now I'm supposed to believe,
    that you ready to play this chess game?

And I'm supposed to forgive and forget,
    they way that you dogged me?

Plus, every ounce of hurt, pain, and misery,
    that you caused me?

You sorry, and you want me to know,
    just how much you miss me?

And you willing to do,
    whatever it takes to convince me?

Whatever needs to be done,
    you want to do to restore this?

You want to get it back,
    to the way that it was before this?

Before you left, before you betrayed me,
    before this nightmare?

Then just go back in time and don't do it,
    you can start right there.

The Block

Did I ask for this misery,
so people can remember me?

Toast to my memory,
and laugh at my tendencies.

Treated it tenderly,
loved it like it was meant to be.

Refused to take sympathy,
just advice off empathy.

Did what I did relentlessly,
not caring if it injured me.

Learned the rules to the industry,
from listening to its employees.

Followed them all religiously,
the code to the inner streets.

From drugging to inner beef,
from anger to inner peace.

I seen what it did for me,
and the stuff that it hid from me.

Also, the things it did to me,
up to the time they sentenced me.

The First and Last Letter

    I got a long letter lying to me. Straight tripping, why she crying to me? In ten years she wasn't trying to see what I'm trying to be. Now out of the blue she scribing to me, telling me she cool and she ain't hiding from me. She think I'm mad, but still she riding with me. Go on to tell me what she trying to be. A half a page of shit that's lying to me. Some old bullshit I ain't trying to read. A half a page how she provide for her seeds. How she work and go to school in the eve, and what has happened since I left the streets. Who all gaffed and who resting in peace. And how her partners send their blessings to me? Followed by a page that got me thinking, "Why the fuck this bitch keep questioning me?" Is being locked up really stressful to me? Has 10 years taught a lesson to me? Is being free gonna bring some pressure to me? And how long before they set my release? Is being locked up kind of helping me sleep? And do I still have a problem with beef? And is getting high really a problem for me? And do I got these niggas following me? Is my temper still a problem for me? That page ended asking is revenge a motto for me?

    And on the third page, what the fuck this girl say? "Is being locked inside this cage help a thorough change?" She still love me is what the words say. I read between the lines and know she lying, but she cold with her word play. She seen my younger brother Thursday and gave him a message for me saying "how she miss me in the worst way." Slid him the number to her home and her work place. Her cellie number and the digits to where her mother stays. Told him "she hope I get her letter in the worst way." Asking him "how I went to jail in the first place?" Went on to say "I need to find God, and learn to pray." I should stop getting high and stop the fighting every day. And how she seen them lay my homies in an early grave. Boo Man, Banks, Smoke, and Mike, and how they're gone away. And if I want to holler at her, she just a phone away. And if my books short, she flipping half a zone a day. And how her brother FED bound for moving bricks of yay. Forgot to mention how that pussy wet and wants to play. Do I remember how I fucked her on those rainy days, while smoking blunts and drinking Hennessy mixed with Ocean Spray? Do I remember what I gave her for her birthday? That's fine and dandy dirty, why she bail in the first place?

    The last page had me tripping, it's a damn shame. I checked the bottom, why the fuck she use my last name? Continued reading through her comedy and mind games. How she gonna be there for me always, that's a crying shame. I had to laugh cause it's the only thing that hides the pain. Truly Yours, Love Always, signed What's Her Name. P.S., her love's forever and that will never change. I been gone ten long calendars that's down the drain. She think I coming home, so writing me ain't nothing strange. If this broad only knew her efforts are all in vain. This ain't the first letter of lies, them bitches all the same. Pop my locker to add it with my other stress and strain, or grab my lighter and put it to it to watch it turn to flames. Don't see no reason to waste my stamps writing a dirty dame. I'm not to blame because she jumped out my car, my ship, and plane. All of the writing in the world for me does not explain, why after ten whole years of silence shit has up and changed? I want to cry like the Temptations because I wish it'd rain. But I'm a thorough bred bitch, I'll never be a lame!

__Who Will Be There__

From the outside looking in,
illusions are possible.

Friends can pretend,
so changing ups really probable.

Associates can be distant,
setting up little obstacles.

Partners can be persistent,
with loyalty that's illogical.

Family members show love,
because they want to appear responsible.

While comrades will give up blood,
because they're there no matter what you do.

Younger Brother

I always thought you'd turn out like me, but now I'm so proud
of you. You didn't follow in my footsteps and do what I do.
You made your own way in life, and I'm so happy for you.
You stayed away from the gangs and the boys in blue. I chose
hustling, while you chose another route. Momma seen the special
in you, that why she put me out. She didn't want me to corrupt
you, with my bad ways. She also didn't want you to see me when
I had bad days. I didn't understand at first, but now it makes sense.
She didn't want both of us dead, or behind a locked fence. One son
in trouble, the other one never seen the streets. One son a monster,
the other one into making beats. I loved the street life, you ain't never
seen it. That's why I'm here and you're there, with nothing but love
between us.

Chess

I look at jail like a chess game, so many pieces, so many moves, so many things I can do. Looking three moves ahead before I touch a piece, it's something sweet even though these prisons beyond belief. Staff members are opposition along with anybody that's competition. Sacrificed my religion from multiple bad decisions, thought I was close to winning, then lost my queen and a bishop. A couple pawns is missing, but I'm still in position, working on check-mate with every piece that's still living. Two knights and a bishop. Two rooks and six pawns, all for one cause, and all getting along. Defeat is out of the question, so I'm open to suggestions, nothing here is impressing, just anger, hate, and depression. So many unanswered questions I ain't wasting my time, I'm just pushing my pawns across the other side of the line. If they make it, they grow up, if they don't it opens the board. I'm ready for war, and six moves away from the door.

Opposites

Without bad luck,
I wouldn't have no luck at all.

Things don't never go as planned,
when I get up I fall.

If anything can go wrong,
for me they probably will.

If there's a plus,
then I get the wrong side of the deal.

When there is compensation,
I always end up with consequences.

Where there is real talk,
I always hear the lies and contradictions.

If I'm first for anything,
somehow, I'll always be last.

Even with all the answers to the test,
somehow, I won't even pass.

Instead of true friends,
I mostly get enemies in disguise.

And instead of being free,
I got sentenced to serve some time.

7-House

Created, born, and raised in the image of God.
But shackled, treated, and walked in the image of a dog.

Is this meant to be my purpose in life?
Or is this just something I have to suffer in my mission of life?

Degraded by my oppressors every chance that they get.
I've seen everything done in slavery except the whips.

All of the mental torture they did and some of the physical.
The slavery rituals and the conditions are miserable.

Separated from loved ones and taken from family.
Punished and prosecuted by the system's insanity.

Consequence after consequence for hustling and gambling.
Got me stuck inside a cell with no way out like an animal.

Secrets

I keep my hopes and dreams to myself, because prison has altered my trust. I don't talk about what I do, those things do not get discussed. If it's spoken to me, you won't find out from speaking to me. I don't know how to tell, secrets remain secret with me. I don't know how to dry snitch, and I don't pass information. I don't believe in starting rumors or holding dumb conversations. I don't care about who is who, and I don't care what they did. I don't care who they is. I only care about self, and those that really show me their love. I don't care if they close to me, and I don't care if they blood. I only trust a chosen few, because their loyalty is proven. That's why my left hand never knows about what my right hand is doing.

Alternate

I handle the stress,
by thinking about past and present events.

The things that I miss,
and all the things I'll never forget.

What I had and what I lost,
and everything in-between.

What I see and what I saw,
and everything that I've seen.

I handle the strain,
by living in the good memories.

The ones that brighten my day,
the ones that pleasure my dreams.

I don't think of reality,
because it's miserable misery.

It's the only way I cope,
to make sure that this doesn't get to me.

Freedom

Everything you allowed me to do, is one of the reasons I'm missing you.
What you put me through, is one of the reasons I'm pissed at you.

The pro's and the con's always match up and equal the bond.
It evens the fund, to make up everything I've become.

The good and the bad, the happy and the sad that I've endured.
The dirty and clean, the watered down and even the pure.

You give and you take, never too much and never enough.
Is the only reason I love and hate my freedom so much.

Education

    If you can learn from a mistake,
does that make mistakes simple lessons?

    Are other people's mistakes,
answers to simple questions?

    Can you learn a lot from a dummy,
or is the dummy the student?

    Will a person that always lies,
ever be seen as truthful?

    After years of misery,
can a person find happiness?

    Should the world be seen in black and white,
as a curse or a gift?

<u>Vision</u>

I seen women act masculine,
      and men act feminine.

I also seen tribes,
      with more chiefs than Indians.

A-whole-lot of big I's,
      and not enough little U's.

A-whole-bunch of bad guys,
      and not enough good dudes.

I seen a lot of drug dealers,
      broke, dusted, and disgusted.

I also seen a bunch of killers,
      that ain't gonna murder nothing.

A-whole-bunch of snitches,
      that get treated like they ain't said nothing.

A-whole-bunch of convicts,
      that get treated like they have said something.

I seen a lot of gangbangers,
      make friends with their enemies.

I also seen players and macks,
      with real jealous tendencies.

And more lames and squares,
      than I could swing a stick at.

I've seen so many characters,
      I've even seen them mismatch.

Know It All

Since you know everything, tell me why you in prison?
How'd you ever catch a case, why you stuck in the system?
Why your books ain't right, why your money ain't straight?
Why you always pan-handling, why you live off the state?
Where the broads that you claim you have, why ain't they riding?
Where your so-called partners at, why is they hiding?
Is everything you say a lie, or are you just bending the truth?
Should I believe a word you say, or should I wait on some proof?
From the looks of things, your conversation is just a hustle.
Because everything you know, ain't really touching on nothing.

Imagination

The system can lock up my body,
but the fences can't hold my mind.

My mind stays on a journey,
that transcends space and time.

The thought was the cause of it all,
thinking it into existence.

Concentrating and focused,
my thought pattern's persistent.

Never facing consequences,
for the mental endeavors.

Imagining real adventures,
that hold pain and pleasure.

Stuck in the past,
chasing the future lost in the present.

So many answers,
it's hard formulating the questions.

I'm here but I'm not,
so close I can see where I want to be.

That's the reason my thoughts run,
because they keep me feeling free.

Comrade

Please forgive me for not being there when you call. I'm surrounded by fences and walls screaming "fuck the law". No blood ties between us but that's misdemeanor. No matter sober or weeded you come when I need you. I count on a thug to show me love no mean mugs. Riding no matter what and ain't never gone give a fuck. We share the same emotions like a roller coaster. Static brought us closer when the time came you was a soldier. Now I'm penitentiary living dealing with twisted feelings. Penalized and repented for every sin I've committed. 18 more months before they set me back. Time moving so slow… I did it all for scratch. Hood love gave me the attitude to hold a grudge. Animosity for the judge that didn't show me love. Every day I open my eyes my mind counts reasons to die. One… to live for my family while doing this. Please forgive me for what I did. I played by the rules…no women, no kids.

Your Worth

I stopped counting the reasons I love you,
because I ran out of numbers.

You're more than a mother,
you're like a big sister and a brother.

You're an auntie and an uncle,
you're a friend and an associate.

You're a teacher and a coach,
you're a banker and a socialist.

Without a father,
you even found the time to play his role.

So you're priceless in the flesh,
And worth more than your weight in gold.

Forgiveness

What can I do to make it right, after all my wrongs? What's taking so long, for you to forgive what I've done? If words ain't enough, what can I do to apologize? What is the bottom line, what will it take to correct my lies? Flowers, candy, and cards, will it take something material? Or do you want the physical, or something that's spiritual? Give me a hint, because the silence confuses me. Do you know what you do to me, I want it back how it used to be. Unconditional love, trust, and intimacy. Everything that I need, everything I gave to receive. I know I was wrong, I know you won't forgive or forget. Just let me repent, I promise it won't happen again.

Present & Past

Stuck inside a bad dream,
    completely out of reality.

Nothing is real to me,
    all of my wishes are casualties.

My hopes are no longer relevant,
    they're stuck in a black hole.

My aspirations have given up,
    to live is their last goal.

I long to do it again,
    to change the places I went wrong.

Praying I get the chance,
    knowing those moments are long gone.

Reminiscing in hindsight,
    surrounded by misery.

Running away from real life,
    lost in a memory.

99 Problems

I got 2 real enemies,
15 that pretend to be,
13 remedies,
and 9 violent tendencies,
8 pending cases,
11 felony charges,
7 witness statements,
and 3 felony lawyers,
6 friends telling,
1 public pretender,
4 bonds posted,
and 12 jury members,
5 guilty verdicts,
+ 3 months on the run.
_____

I got 99 problems, but a bitch ain't one!

The Institution

There ain't no love in the system, just arguments and whispers. Speaking of the business, and everything that's lost to their prisons.

So many days and years, that it's hard to add them up. Punishment after punishment, so much like they're mad at us.

Chained, cuffed, and shackled, to degrade while they torture us. Trapped behind the fences, by wizards and sorcerers.

Stuck with nowhere to go, or place to hide to escape it all. Consequences after consequences, for losing while trying to ball.

Actual Friend

I need a friend that understands my pain.
I need a friend that understands when I have stress and strain.
I need a friend to be around when I need them or not.
I need a friend to be around if it is cold or it's hot.
I need a friend to tell the truth to me and never lie.
I need a friend to boost my spirit if it's low or it's high.
I need a friend to show me sympathy for things that I've been through.
I need a friend to show me empathy for things that they've been through.
I need a friend to be a friend that loves me unconditionally.
I need a friend that loves me for who I am, not who they want me to be.

EJS

I think about you every day,
and not a day goes by…

You stay inside my thoughts,
every day you cross my mind.

I love you,
with all my heart, mind, body and soul…

Whatever you do,
whatever you say, and wherever you go.

You stay on my mind,
at all different times of day…

You're my everything,
and I don't want it no other way.

Clarity

My definition of a friend, is the one that cares.
The one that's fair, the person that is always there.

My definition of a friend, is the one that's strong.
The one that's home, the person there through
right and wrong.

My definition of a friend, is the one that listens.
The one that whispers, the person I can tell my wishes.

My definition of a friend, is the one that's true.
The one that's blue, my definition of a friend is you…

Silence

Give me a moment to think,
without a sound or movement to interfere.

Give me a chance to understand and see,
that I'm really here.

Taken away from family, friends,
and people that's really near.

Praying nobody leaves me,
because that is one of my biggest fears.

Conversation

If I offended you,
    then let me apologize.
Let's sit down and talk,
    until we see where the problem lies.

There's no reason for this,
    to interfere with our pleasantness.
There's no reason for words,
    to break up our togetherness.

Whatever it is, whatever happened,
    there's a way to fix it.
Through conversation, through correspondence,
    through handling business.

Where there's a will, there's a way,
    as long as we can agree.
To handle issues like adults,
    and not like kids on the streets.

Love One

Got me telling momma about the drama, praying love will
last. Chose the wrong path, oldest of two boys she had.
Bad seed start blowing weed right after momma conceived.
My younger brother in her time of need, I'm running the streets.
"Fuck the world", how I felt; can't understand why she bothered.
Bullshit hand I was dealt turn out just like my father.
Momma told me, but I didn't listen, steady going on missions.
"I'd be dead or in jail by 21". I thought she was tripping.
142 ran into 20 years. Second time momma came to tears so I
ain't happy here. Burned, stabbed, shot up and still in it.
I thank momma for raising a soldier that's still living.
I ain't never apologized with watered eyes but realize.
Collect calls and visits my only way of repentance. Momma
I'm sorry for pain I put you through. Last letter told me she loved
me and I love her too…

Assurance

Promises
are
only
as
good
as
the
moments
they
were
made.

Making
those
moments
meaningful
memories.

Everyday

Some days are bad days,
    most days are worse than others.

No days are good days,
    they're a mixture of one another.

Some days are full of stress,
    most days are full of frustrations.

No days are happy ones,
    they're a mixture of aggravations.

Some days are completely hopeless,
    most days are a constant struggle.

No days are completely peaceful,
    they're a mixture of different troubles.

Some days I want to give up,
    most days I don't even care.

No days I want to remember,
    they're a mixture of real despair.

Friend

Now I'm counting the days my comrade, confined in jail cells. I been there and done that so I know it's hell. Circumstances brought us together that we couldn't avoid. Whipping pills of P-funk scoy mad and popping toys. Aggravating the situation drug addicted and tripping. I'm in the pen while you waiting on consequences. Conversing through mail call expressing feelings of anger. I feel your pain player just hold on…. This 20 years a major bid life without even worse. Repercussions that hurt but we had to put in the work. Selling amphetamines chasing dreams too far out to reach. Serving fiends collecting green brought down by the streets. Now I'm speaking of love loss "fuck the world" what you preaching. Raised by different teachers but in my eyes we equals. Separate fathers and mothers but brother we still kin. Related by sin playing this game to win.

Love Bird

Through all the pain,
you've been with me like the swan that you is.

Through all that I've did,
you're by my side every place that I've been.

You hold my soul delicately,
but firm enough to show love.

You're all the above,
and care enough for me not to judge.

Your qualities,
are like the pedals of a rose in the summer.

One after another,
the layers of a friendship and lover.

Your love is the key,
that works to open the lock on my heart.

And with your support,
we'll get through all the time we're apart.

Pain

I see my death with each and every breath,
each and every step,
each and every test,
each and every stress.

While most dying to live I'm living to die,
cursed with the time,
reversing the time,
so now I'm not too certain of time.

What's worse than dying,
is living with no purpose inside,
or getting caught up on emotions and pride.

The only thing that brings a tear to my eye,
is each and every time my mother has cried,
because her pain is all that hurts me inside.

Wisdom

In my search for love and compassion,
    I must have had it backwards.

Because instead of attraction,
    I found hatred and detraction.

I got lost in the lies,
    confused about what's real and what ain't.

Who real and who ain't.
    confused about what's real and what's fake.

Was it love or infatuation,
    that gave me the inspiration.

That gave me the piece of patience,
    to deal with the irritations.

The ups and the downs the in-betweens,
    the lows and the highs.

The shock and surprise,
    that went with all the truths and the lies.

I made a mistake when I thought I had it made,
    but I didn't.

I was blindly addicted,
    and didn't know that I was the victim.

When I found out the truth,
    it was too late to fix my affliction.

There was nothing that could be done,
    to right the wrong contradictions.

I tried and I failed,
    I loved but didn't get none in return.

But I wouldn't change it for nothing,
    because of the lessons I learned.

Where's the Love

I never thought coming to jail would bring my family down. But I learned that love isn't love when people don't stay around. They're there when it's good and claim that they'll be loyal and down. But when things ain't going their way they ain't nowhere to be found. Out of sight, out of mind, the kind that just show love when they see you. They love when they need you, and when they don't, they hate and deceive you. They're family and friends on the surface, underneath they're the enemy. The ones that pretend to be there, but they got traitorous tendencies. Their love isn't genuine, it's built on selfish intentions. It's full of conditions, exceptions, and some petty restrictions. With time it gets worse and worse, farther away from what's perfect. It's useless to work it, when their lack of love is on purpose. It hurts to accept it, especially when it's so disrespectful. And no matter how you reject it, the dots become too hard to connect them. The harder you try, the more problems you have in the end. Dealing with life in the pen, when friends and family members pretend.

Water

      If I could cry from all this pain,
I'd shed a river of tears.

      Living here for more than ten,
can make a river a year.

      Every opportunity missed,
every chance I ain't get.

      Every time I wanted to split,
but got stopped by the fence.

      The pain is constant,
to the point that it hurts just to breathe.

      Every breath is a little more,
knowing right now I can't leave.

      There's some light at the end,
but when is not for me to decide.

      So I keep tears in my eyes that won't fall,
no matter how hard I try.

<u>Perception</u>

More than a decade in hindsight,
    I never would have made this mistake.

Would have never made that mistake,
    to get me stuck in this place.

    Would have never made those mistakes,
        to get me stuck with this case.

        I would have never traded freedom,
            for a stay with the state.

History

What does it mean to be free,
when all I see is gun towers and prison fences?

Years of consequences,
for the street life competitions.

Family members passing,
while fake friends keep popping up.

Women coming and going,
while their timing is unpopular.

Money funny as comedy,
and hustling is a lost art.

Tough guys in abundance,
and the real is a lost thought.

Faking is the usual,
and word games are the regular.

Guards on power trips,
with lousy dudes for competitors.

Every day is the same,
along with every week, month, and year.

My definition of freedom,
is the time that I wasn't here.

<u>Momma</u>

My love is unconditional,
      no matter what the condition is.

I love you for where you are going,
      where you're at, and where you've been.

Everything I got was from you,
      So I honor you for those gifts.

Everything I asked for you gave,
      so you're part of a granted wish.

You love me the way I love you,
      whether I'm right or wrong.

You carried me when I needed help,
      showing me that you're strong.

You're always there in my time of need,
      whenever I've needed you.

So I love you more than infinity,
      simply for being you.

Recidivist

Sitting in a cell questioning self about why I did that. Watching time fly on some days I will never get back.

Physical torture limited, mental anguish is limitless. Warehoused from prison to prison is the truth behind what their business is.

No rehabilitation or programs to help me learn something. Besides some more criminal ways I really ain't learned nothing.

I'm worse than when I came and I feel like I have a death wish. Prison bred to come back with more time than I left with.

Prison

I can hear the walls talking, so I'm humbly listening. Telling me what the business is, so low that they whispering. Concrete conversations, breaking down my predicament. Explaining every trial and tribulation that I'm living with. From guilty to innocent, from outer in inner sense. From debts to benefits, from loyal to benedict. Colder than the winter is, with stress that seems limitless. Trapped inside of a killer fence, with no way off the premises. This life is a gift and curse, with more hurt than a little bit. With more ifs and buts, on what I could've and should've did.

Lady Abstract

I never felt this way before, so this feeling is really new to me. Truthfully, I'm falling in love with the things you do to me. The things you do for me, are the definition of kindness. I was looking for love, and you showed me the way to find it. Our trials and tribulations have passed, now they're behind us. I can define trust, with the same words that describe us. But words can't even describe, the way that you make me feel now. I wanted to let it go, you're the reason I want to live now. You showed me a different side of life, besides all of my loneliness. You showed me that I could make it, because I didn't really know my strength. You tell me "that it will be okay", when I didn't think it will be. I thought that I was fine alone, but having you fulfills me. There are so many things I want to say, but I don't know where to start at. Regardless of where I am, with you is where my heart's at.

First, allow me to thank you, for giving me motivation. For giving me inspiration, to deal with my situation. I wish that I could explain to you, how having you has changed me. Strangely, I know that I never will be the same me. The old me is long gone, he left after I found you. Everything is different, I'm not the same when I'm around you. We can talk about anything; our conversations are beautiful. We can exchange secrets, or just speak about the usual. I'm comfortable in my skin with you, I don't have to pretend. And as my feelings ascend, it makes it easy loving a friend. I can share with you all my hopes and dreams, knowing you'll never judge me. Share with you how I really feel, knowing the way you love me.

I feel the same way about you and love you more than you'll ever know. You'll never know, no matter how many times that I tell you so. Words can never describe the way I feel, no matter what I say. Ove lay our yay, I really do in every way. And I ish way hat tay, I could show you how much I mean it. So ou yay now kay, there is nothing but love between us.

I thought I lost you forever, but luckily you came back to me. I pray that we last forever, so there's never a person after me. I'm ready to be committed, I'm ready for a relationship. I'm ready to make it work, no matter where we end up taking it. I'll give as you give, take as you take, unconditionally. Love as you love, and even miss you how you missing me. I'll love you for who you are, and not the person I wish you'd be. Forever and ever I promise, and a promise is meant to keep.

Made in United States
Orlando, FL
13 March 2024

44739163R00046